6 Months To 655 Units

"How to break into multifamily investing with no capital and all social media"

By Will Morris

v1.5

Copyright © 2019 Will Morris Publications

All Rights Reserved.

No part of this book may be reproduced in any form or by any electronic or mechanical means, including information storage and retrieval systems, without permission in writing from the author. The only exception is by a reviewer, who may quote short excerpts in a published review.

ISBN: 9781689764223

The information presented herein represents the view of the author as of the date of publication. This book is presented for informational purposes only. Due to the rate at which conditions change, the author reserves the right to alter and update his opinions based on new conditions. While every attempt has been made to verify the information in this book, neither the author nor his affiliates/partners assume any responsibility for errors, inaccuracies, or omissions.

This Book Is Given To:

_____

Because I Care About Your Success and Financial Future

Free Bonuses

As a thank you for reading this book, *6 Months To 655 Units*, and committing yourself to financial freedom and taking control of your future, I've put together some excellent tools and resources that's helped me and I know will help you.

I'm giving you a:

- Posting Schedule
- Accountability Schedule
- Content Creation Guide

Theses Free PDF's are $829 worth of bonuses...

Send email with subject *re: book bonuses*

info@heyWillMorris.com

Free Bonuses 5

Preface 11

Introduction 15

CHAPTER. 1 21

Seeing Opportunity 21

CHAPTER. 2 27

How It Works 27

CHAPTER. 3 35

Branding 35

CHAPTER. 4 41

Gaining Attention 41

CHAPTER 5 47

Social Media Strategy 47

    The Basics 49

    Facebook 49

    LinkedIn... 52

    YouTube 53

    Content, Content, Content............................. 54

    Why Does This Work 56

CHAPTER 6 .... **59**

    The Greatest Showman 59

CHAPTER 7 .... **67**

    The Capital Raise... 67

    What I learned 69

    The Hidden Benefit... 70

CHAPTER 8 .... **73**

What's Next 73

    Free Bonuses 76

    Looking For More? 77

Additional Resources 79

Book Will To Speak 81

Final Thought 83

Preface

6 Months To 655 Unit

Will Morris has been involved with multifamily assets for over 8 years. In just 6 months, Will Morris went from 0 to in the GP on 655 units totaling almost 28 million in real estate  by leveraging social media to gain attention and raise capital. Prior to Will being in the GP on 655 units, he had supplied over 3,000 units for the value-added from import and domestic manufacturers. Will now focuses on growing his real estate portfolio through syndicating great cash flowing assets and sharing his knowledge to help others to financial freedom.

As this book goes to press, Will has transitioned into acquiring his own assets with his companies Morris

Acquisitions and Trifecta Equity Partners, as well as partnering with others in their deals.

Bedsides building his portfolio, Will still uses his system to achieve his second burning desire, to relieve people of Finacle burden by showing them they too with hard work and determination can achieve financial freedom. Understanding that people consume information in different forms, Will has created online and in-person training and events workshops where people who seek financial freedom through real estate can learn the step-by-step system he uses.

Introduction

6 Months To 655 Unit

As long as I can remember, I have desired Finacle freedom for myself and the people I meet. I have always been very entrepreneur minded and I have always tried to figure out new ways to solve problems or make life better. In my career I have started, grown, excited and failed several businesses.

After I graduated high school, I tried college for a while but could not attend the classes as required. I was too interested in my entrepreneurial endeavors. Instead I set out to set the world on fire with no real direction. I literally would discover something new and start a business pursuing this new discovery. Along the way I developed a love for learning, reading, and studying. I just wanted to consume information. I've spent the past 8 years on a double path, one is an epic journey learning and studying and the other is my career in multifamily.

On one path I've read hundreds of books, spent tens of thousands of dollars on courses, workshops, and bootcamps. I've deep dove into social marketing, self-improvement, financial literacy, and selling.

The other path was hands-on working closely with acquisition teams. With my thirst for knowledge and passion for multifamily this hands-on education reshaped my life.

It wasn't until these two paths finally crossed that I noticed my greatest opportunity yet and gave me my shot at my true desire of doing my own deals. What's crazy is that if I had not been studying all those things and being educated in multifamily at the same time, I would not have been aware or noticed this opportunity and would not be able to share it with you today.

I was inspired to write this book after discovering, implementing and proving my system and methods to being successful in real estate. I knew that if I could do this, I knew others can too and I'm obligated to share what I have created.

6 Months To 655 Unit

CHAPTER. 1

Seeing Opportunity

6 Months To 655 Unit

Seeing Opportunity

I started in multifamily as a general contractor doing the value-add turns for large multifamily owners. I always watched and measured the time it took my crews to complete the task required involved in the rehabs. At best they could turn a unit in about a week. However, I noticed the cabinet and granite countertops companies would drop off 10-20 units' worth of material one day each month. Trust me, I know because they would just drop their loads in the parking lot and I would have to deal with it. I got to thinking *"they are working one day a month and invoicing for 20+ units, that's what I need to be doing"*. I started researching how to supply large rehabs, I found out about manufacture direct, and importing. I discovered I must get my customs ID, insurance, and learn the documents required to start importing. So, I did, and the transition happened from contracting the rehabs to supplying the rehabs. *(I have found it best to hire help for the paperwork end of importing, you don't want to get it wrong, its expensive.)* I immediately went back to the owners I had been working for and asked to quote their next value add. I lost the first few bids, then "BOOM" winner. With this new proof of concept, I continued to bid on projects and in no time, I was supplying components for value add across the entire US from import and domestic manufactures. Just when things were going well, hello problem. I had several projects going on at the same time and due to having to cover a small spread on the payments to the manufacture, I was running out of money. As a potential solution I offered to broker (cost plus) the components. This would lower my clients cost and help take the financial burden off me.

Seeing Opportunity

The hidden benefit of this decision soon revealed itself, unknowingly it allowed me to see my client's syndication process and deal numbers. I asked questions, why this property, why not that property, how did you get that number, what does this number mean, after a while, I began to understand. I furthered my own study of the process, syndication, debt, equity, investors, GP, LLC, etc. Meanwhile, my knowledge and skill in the social, branding, marketing, selling, financial literacy, and self-improvement were advancing rapidly. As my awareness and knowledge of both industries grew, I discovered a new opportunity. As I had several times before, I jumped into this new opportunity with both feet. Which has set me on my new path of syndicating my own deals, building my network, joining others as GP on their deals, and raising capital. Now, I'm continuing to push forward in my newfound love and passion in my career. The benefits of owning multifamily will only be understood by some as most think it's unattainable. I encourage you to watch, learn and study from the mover and shakers in multifamily investing because if I can do this, I know you can too.

CHAPTER. 2

How It Works

6 Months To 655 Unit

How It Works

I've noticed a recent trend in the real estate world. I first noticed it in residential, wholesalers are working themselves into the deal by focusing on one aspect of the process. It looks like this, flippers spend all their time focused on fixing/flipping the house therefore they lack deal flow. Wholesalers spend all their time marketing and finding deals to assign to the flippers. This is working themselves into the deal. I call it thier *"specialized focus of activity"*. The progression seems after fees accumulate, wholesalers are ready to do their own flipping and they get to cherry-pick the houses they find. Once they get too deep in flipping, the cycle starts over again.

Take multifamily, there's another trend I've noticed, and it comes from the JOBS Act in 2012. A little history lesson here: "The Jumpstart Our Business Act, or JOBS Act is a law intended to encourage funding of small businesses in the United States by easing many of the country's securities regulations. More Specifically Title II - Accredited Crowdfunding pursuant to Title II of the JOBS Act and Rule 506(c) promulgated under the Securities Act of 1933 (the "Act"), also called "accredited crowdfunding" has no restrictions on the type of general solicitations that may be made or the media that may be employed to make such solicitations. This means that a company raising funds via accredited crowdfunding (an "issuer") is free to use Facebook, Twitter, LinkedIn, YouTube, and any other medium to advertise, describe and generate buzz about the offering. While this seems broad and is nothing less than a revolutionary change in this country's securities laws, there are certain considerations that an issuer must know of and precautions it must take.

How It Works

Your traditional and existing multifamily investment firms and syndicators are so focused on charts, growth, numbers, and figures, which are all very important and you must know to be successful in this business, are not paying attention to the changes in raising capital due to the JOBS act. Same as before if I put my specialized focus of activity on raising capital through these newly added avenues and you spend all your time on operations, who is going to raise more capital?

Secondly, the traditional investors and syndicators are used to working their existing network of investors to raise capital to take down deals. The problem with this method is you're restricted by how many people you know and how deep their pockets are. No problem if you know Warren Buffet, but for most, this is a problem. That's where social media and Title II of the JOBS Act weighs in. What social media does and how it allows you to beat the competition is it gives you distribution and scale which you don't have with traditional network capital raising.

Within this is where yet again I saw my next opportunity. Traditional owners, operators and syndicators don't know how to communicate nor use modern techniques to raise capital. They don't know how to leverage social media, which gives you distribution and scale. I knew that if I could use social media to raise capital, I could get what I wanted out of the deal, control the capital control the deal. Because I was started from nothing I had to break out of obscurity and distinguish myself as an (*authority in the field*) I was going to use social media to raise capital by (*educating*) what investors can do with their money in multifamily deals this helps to (*gain attention*). This (*show and tell*) strategy would also (influence) investors by (*giving value*) first, therefore (*attracting*) not (*chasing*) them. I call this my double door strategy. By the time I had the (*attention*) of about 2.3 million dollars, I also had the attention of traditional syndicators with good deals. The syndicators contacted me about helping them on their deals, I demanded a 2% upfront acquisitions fee and a 20% profit share on the backend of the deal. They may have owned the bull, but I had it by the horns.

6 Months To 655 Unit

CHAPTER. 3

Branding

6 Months To 655 Unit

Branding

After writing this book, traveling speaking, and teaching my methods. I realized that what I am sharing is much more powerful than just methods. I am showing people how to in modern times, break through obscurity, distinguish themselves, and become an authority in their space. I would like to add as you read the following chapters, be thinking about YOU. What makes you unique? Where do you come from? How were you raised? What experiences did you have that make you who you are today? What is your story?

"The reality is, at the end of the day, any and everything we try to do in life, has probably already been done. The only thing different about what YOU are doing is YOU."

– Will Morris

For example, how would you start a coffee cup business in 2020, since there are so many coffee cups? The only hope would be your branding. You would have to distinguish your coffee cup business from every other coffee cup in the world. YOU would have to do this through YOUR story. Your story might be that your cups are made of tin because when you were fighting in the Vietnam war you always drank coffee from a tin cup. You remember how the tin cup always keep your coffee just the right temp as you drank it. Not to hot not to cold, just right. You always enjoyed that small moment of happiness even though you were in a war. Now you want to share that same moment of happiness with everyone each morning as they drink form your tin coffee cup.

See how I tied the story into emotion then into the customer. No one will have the same experience the same way you do. Fact is two people can experience something together, but both will have a different

Branding

experience. You must keep this in mind throughout this book and into your future, no matter what your path is. When its all said and done all we have is our story and how we experienced it. This is the key to breaking though obscurity, which at the root of it, is what this book is all about.

6 Months To 655 Unit

CHAPTER. 4

Gaining Attention

6 Months To 655 Unit

Gaining Attention

In modern times, you must think, treat, and act as if you and your investment are a media company. You must promote and advertise as if your investment is a headlining show. One of my favorite books by Eugene Schwartz - Breakthrough Advertising - *Let's get to the heart of the matter. The power, the force, the overwhelming urge to own that makes advertising work, comes from the market itself, and not from the copy. Copy cannot create desire for a product. It can only take the hopes, dreams, fears and desires that already exists in the hearts of millions of people and focus those already existing desires onto a particular product. This is the copy writer's task: not to create this mass desire – but to channel and direct it.*

You want to take all the existing hope, dreams, fears and desires and turn their focus to you. You become their vehicle to those desires and their leader around their fears. You should be telling everyone about the benefits your investment offers. Don't talk numbers at first, talk benefits. Think of your investment opportunity as a product. The physical part of your product is of value only because it enables your product to do things for people. The important part of your product is what it does. What your investors are really paying you for is what the product will do for them.

Networking, events, phone calls and daily activities you want to document and share it all. If you meet someone, ask to film or audio record your meeting for a mutual benefit. Set up times for phone calls where you can record the conversation. Think as if you are an investment magazine tying to share as much as you can about multifamily investing. You want to become their go-to source for advice and information. Write a book, start a show, start doing events, start a podcast, you MUST create a vehicle for yourself that puts you as an authority in you space.

This may be a shocker to some of you. You want to give it all, give all the knowledge, gold nuggets and hidden gems you have. Your best secrets, tips and even tricks with no return expected. I can imagine most of your jaws just dropped, but this is where most fail. There will come a time to ask for the sell if you even have to but now is not it.

This is the method of ATTRACTING not chasing.

6 Months To 655 Unit

CHAPTER 5

Social Media Strategy

6 Months To 655 Unit

Social Media Strategy

The Basics

The two references below will get you started, which is what you need to do, just get started. They are similar on each platform but may very a little.

- # - refers to a topic. Ex. #life, #realestate
- @ - refers to a person. Ex. @heyWillMorris

Ex post. Watch @heyWillMorris show you how to break out of #obscurity, and #distinguish yourself as an #authority.

Facebook

Join groups with a multifamily focus. Share what you're doing, (*what you're doing and give actionable advice*). Share your knowledge and experience. Post something funny, we all love funny stuff, but don't go comedian on them, you want to still keep the focus multifamily.

Follow the mover and shakers in multifamily on social networks. You may not agree with what they are preaching or "selling" but they have the spotlight and you want to gain some of that attention. After you follow these "social gurus" watch for a post from them getting a lot of comments and shares. Post a comment on that post, direct it to the guru but in public view where everyone can see it. What happens, these gurus have so much attention they can't get to (*service*) all of their followers. Human nature is they want to be close to the leader, however, this "leader" isn't giving them the attention they want. So, when you comment, not being rude or selling, you direct some of their follower's attention to you. The guru's followers think, this guy or gal knows what they're talking about, I'll follow him/her to see if they will give me the attention I want.

Social Media Strategy

For example, how I discovered this. A "guru" that I was following posted a Facebook live video of him walking through a community his team has under contract talking about the value-add opportunities within that asset. I got a notification he was live, and I clicked to watch the post. I noticed all the comments he was getting to ask about investing with him and the expected returns. I thought I would like his attention right now to talk about the 244 units I just got under contract too. Without thinking, I posted this comment "hey _____ I just got 244 units in _____ would you want to partner with me?" that's it. What happened next was nothing less than eye-opening. Not only did I get recognized by this "guru," it really nicely blew me off by saying "yeah just send to my acquisitions guy at _____" which was also a plug for himself. I also got reply comments "I'm interested" and "how can I learn more". I quickly sent them Private Messages because I realized I just stole his spotlight and I didn't want to miss the opportunity. That one comment ended up in a

$500,000.00 commitment and set up several more introductions that became great relationships.

LinkedIn

This is the Facebook for professionals. Here you need to be posting videos because no one else seems to want to. You need to be writing LinkedIn articles don't matter the length. Something you can do is record a video, post it, then write exactly what you just said in the video in an article (*repurpose content*). People consume content in different ways, so you want to be there for however they feel most comfortable consuming. You want to be educating, helpful and giving free value.

For example, I was at a property, a 98-unit value add opportunity, I had been trying to get under contract for years. I decided to pull out my phone and record myself talking about the value add I would do to the property, why I would do it and what potential cost concerns I would be looking for within that project. Mainly I was doing this because I was waiting for the property manager to get there for me to ask if they were ready to sell yet. However, in a short 5 min video, that I thought wasn't anything really important because it all seems second nature, I apparently shared some valuable information. That post trended on LinkedIn, I added over 100 great connections and scheduled several meetings for the next 3 weeks.

YouTube

It's important because it is owned by Google which means it's tied into just about every kind of internet search-related inquiry. As the owner, Google wants to promote their own platforms first. In turn, Google will show their own platforms first or rank them higher in search inquiries.

YouTube is a place for longer videos. YouTube ranks their videos on watch time. Your longer form videos will add up to a longer watch time and thus a better video ranking.

At the time of this book, YouTube is in a great place to promote. Google is wanting to take market share from other advertising platforms, so they are incentivizing people to promote. For example, they only charge you if someone clicks on your promoted video or watches 30 seconds or more. This is important because you may have 10k views at 29 seconds and not cost you anything, but you still got exposed to 10k viewers.

Content, Content, Content

First, let me set a few ground rules for content.

1. Be worth watching. This can be done by the following:
    a. Educate
    b. Entertain

Social Media Strategy

   c. Engage
2. DON'T SELL. If you get the 1.2 seconds of attention of a prospect for the first time, you DON'T want to ruin it by trying to sell them.
   a. Fall back on #1 rule
   b. Give Value at least 3 to 5 times before making an offer or trying to sell.
   c. Best of all, try to help them first, then they feel obligated to help you back.
3. You must be consistent. You must be in front of mind and you must be easily available when your prospect is ready to interact with you.
   a. Make a posting schedule and treat it as an appointment you can't miss.
   b. Reuse content.
      i. Ex.: Shoot a video for YouTube, pull audio for a podcast, transcribe audio into blog or article, and cut short clips of video for a post like on Instagram.

This is where most of you will fail and why most of you won't be able to gain attention and raise capital via social media. It's a lot of work and its hard and unless you have a lot of money to pay people to do it for you, it's time-consuming. I didn't have the money, but I did and still have the drive and ambition to become a real estate mogul. You will need that same drive to stay consistent, dedicated and disciplined. If you do, if you're willing to put in the work, it will distinguish you from everyone else that's not willing to put in the work and set you as an authority in your space. You will become successful, happy and financially free, you must decide if it's worth it and how bad you want it.

Why Does This Work

It all goes back to how we as people have consumed content and been taught over the years. Here's the science behind this strategy.

Think about your schooling, in school you would sit down in a room as a teacher stood in front of you, presenting to you. The teacher or educator would teach on a subject from a book or what they learned themselves as you watched. You would ask the teacher questions, they would engage with you and answer them, or the teacher would know your question beforehand and answer it.

Think about watching TV. When you watch the news, you're normally sitting in a room watching the news anchors as they give you information and educate you on what's happening. Your favorite TV show or movie is entertaining you from a screen you watch.

This is all the same pattern you watch someone either in person or on a screen and you associate them as an expert or a celebrity. You are attracted to them, admire them and want to follow them.

The same thing happens now but it's through your phone and computers in posts, webinars, videos, and LIVE events.

CHAPTER 6

The Greatest Showman

6 Months To 655 Unit

The Greatest Showman

You will become a great showman. You will have the attention and spotlight on you. Once you have gained this attention, you'll build influence, be able to direct and persuade people's attention in any direction you desire.

Think of any show, you pay to see the finished act, what you don't see is all the behind the scenes that goes into making the show. Your audience, no matter if it's the church watching the preacher, watching a YouTube video, going to Disney World, or going to see a Broadway play, everyone shows up and spends their hard-earned dollar for the finished show. We as humans want to be entertained. Just to drive it home, think of Jay Leno vs all the teachers in California. Jay at one time made more money than all the teachers in the state of California combined. I'm not saying you must become a movie star or late-night show host, but you need to be the finished show. If you want to leverage attention to work yourself into deals this is the path. I'm not political but look at our president, he leveraged attention to win the race, *attention is the new currency*. Plus, you might land some speaking gigs, a book deal, or start your own coaching program which would all help make more money to pour back into real estate.

Now the good news, you don't have to do this all by yourself. Actually, I recommend not doing this by yourself. You must be focused on finding deals, finding capital, gaining attention and selling your products or courses if the opportunity presents itself. What you need to do is focus on being the greatest showman and get others to do the grunt work. Below are some places to start with outsourcing.

Examples of outsourcing:

1. Hire or partner with a social marketing company to help you with social advertising. You can offer them a profit share of the deals or a percentage of capital raised.
2. Find private label right articles and content you can use in your posts, articles, and blogs. With private label content you can reuse and publish as if you created it, put your name on it and rebrand it.
3. Use sites like Upwork.com and Fiverr.com to outsource your time-consuming tasks. I recommend the video editing, video intros, article writing, graphic designs, data entry, data scraping, technical issues and anything else that takes time and skill. You can literally find someone to do just about anything on those sites.

Invest in yourself. Buy an investing course, go to an investing workshop, buy and read investing books. You must invest in your own knowledge. Get a nice-looking suit, not an expensive suit. My first suit was a $199 coat and pants special from Kohls and I made at least $100,000 in that suit.

Don't think you need to buy a Lambo unless you have a local Lambo club that has high net worth members, then I would consider it. Think about taking photos with Lambos and airplanes all the things you see the mover and shakers doing. Yes, it's corny but remember, you're not creating desire, you're just directing that existing desire to you or your product. Meaning that investor's desires are to be wealthy and have a Lambo and a jet. You are aligning their vision of success and wealth with your projected messaging, so they're attracted to you. You want to parallel with the conversation that's going on inside your audience's head. Think back to the greatest showman. The audience is paying to see the finished show "you";

The Greatest Showman

people are interested in the destination more than the trip to the destination.

6 Months To 655 Unit

CHAPTER 7
The Capital Raise

6 Months To 655 Unit

The Capital Raise

Once you have their attention, become the greatest showman, and built authority in your space. It comes time to bring home the cash, deliver on your commitment to your syndicators, and stake your claim in the deal.

What I learned

Ask your syndicator how do they plan to receive funds? I discovered that some syndicators have strategies to create urgency and scarcity within their deals. I didn't know that. I had a guy looking to invest $500,000 and when I tried to set up the funding transfer, my syndicator partner said they are not taking funds until this date about 30 days later. I said he has $500,000 and he has only 25 days to invest or be fined $40,000, can we not take his money? What I discovered is that there are two common ways to take capital.

1. You have a set date that capital will be taken. Up to that date you get a written capital commitment from your investors.
2. You have an escrow account set up to where you have the investor wire capital to. In this option, you normally pay a small interest on the money to your investors similar to how the bank pays you for your money in your checking account.

The Hidden Benefit

If you remember, you are a capital partner for the syndicator. Meaning you bring the capital for their deal and they handle the rest. This is where I found a hidden benefit when it came to actually transfer capital. Once I had an investor, I would set up a three-way call between myself, the investor and my syndicator partner. This is very similar to the buddy close, a closing technique used in selling. On that call I would introduce everyone and allow my syndicator partner to take the lead explaining the details because, to be honest, they knew it front to back, it was their deal. Once the investor was ready to commit, I handed them off to my syndicator partner to handle the transfer, paperwork, legal, K-1's, etc.

NOTE:

I would advise trying your best to still help your syndicator partner with this process. Because you want to see what their processes are and how they structure it. You want to learn the rest of the syndication process. You will need this soon.

6 Months To 655 Unit

CHAPTER 8

What's Next

6 Months To 655 Unit

What's Next

You will need to know the full process of syndicating. You should know it doesn't mean you should do it. Now you are ready to start building your own team to start syndicating your own properties. You want to find experts in their field for underwriting, acquisitions, dispositions, debt, insurance, and legal. Your goal here is to build a team that will support you as what I call the hunter. You are the one out hunting for deals, gaining attention, as the attractive character. After you find or attract a deal or investor, your team should be able to handle everything else. This is truly the goal. To have a team that is a well-oiled machine. This is where and how your big-time mover and shakers in this industry make it to the top. As you will soon one day too....

Free Bonuses

As a thank you for reading this book *6 Months To 655 Units* and committing yourself to financial freedom and taking control of your future, I've put together some excellent tools and resources that's helped me and I know will help you as well.

I'm giving you a:

- Posting Schedule
- Accountability Schedule
- Content Creation Guide

Theses Free PDF's are $829 worth of bonuses...

Send email with subject *re: book bonuses*

info@heyWillMorris.com

What's Next

Looking For More?

I want to thank you for being one of the readers of this book.

However, one common message that I tend to receive is... **the desire for more**.

Which I'm not surprised, what I lay out in this book is just scraping the surface when it comes to real estate investing, launching Funds, leveraging social media, breaking through obscurity, and gaining attention. As well as the desire to get around and network with like-minded people.

If you would like to learn more about my private equity funds, or hedge funds and investing alongside myself. I encourage you to visit the link below to schedule a call with myself.

https://calendly.com/willmorris/investintrocall

6 Months To 655 Unit

What's Next

Additional Resources

www.business.facebook.com - This is the business manager side of Facebook and where you will create pages and run your advertising for Facebook and Instagram

www.Clickfunnels.com - This is where you will build your sales funnels

www.Upwork.com - This is where you can find people to outsource to

www.Fiverr.com - Another location for outsourcing (shorter easier projects)

www.Linkedin.com - The Professional social platform. At the time of this book a great place to build authority quickly.

www.Twitter.com - More of a short post update style social platform.

www.Instagram.com - A visual social platform, great pictures do well here

www.Canva.com - A tool with templates for social content

www.Adobe.com – Programs for editing your content.

www.heyWillMorris.com – My personal website where you can find courses, programs, and mentoring.

www.Morris3rdCapital.com – My fund management company.

www.MorrisAcquisitions.com – My mobile home, business M&A, and general syndications and acquisitions company.

What's Next

Book Will To Speak

Book Will to speak as your next keynote speaker and you're assured to maximize the value to your audience. Will is the cutting edge for innovating in branding, mindset, capital sourcing and modern real estate.

For more information, please:

Send email with subject *re: book Will to speak*

info@heyWillMorris.com

6 Months To 655 Unit

What's Next

Final Thought

If I was able to help you with this book. If you got anything out of this book, if you took a single note, or I was able to shift your thinking, and most important, if I inspired you in any way, I'm hoping you will do something for me.

Give a copy to someone else.

Share with them how this book added value to you and ask them to read it if they value financial freedom through real estate.

We owe it to ourselves. I need you. Spread the word.

Kindly,

Will Morris

6 Months To 655 Unit

www.ingramcontent.com/pod-product-compliance
Lightning Source LLC
Chambersburg PA
CBHW070812220526
45466CB00002B/642